USING STORIES

KEY STAGE 2 Y5–6/ P6–7

FRANCES MACKAY

Contents

✦ Introduction	3
✦ Novels	4
✦ Classic fiction	10
✦ Playscripts	16
✦ Fairy tales	22
✦ Fables	28
✦ Stories from different cultures	34
✦ Stories of different genres	40
✦ Comparative stories	46
✦ Character studies	52
✦ Stories by the same author	58

Published by Hopscotch Educational Publishing Company Ltd, 8 Severn Close, Leamington Spa CV32 7BZ.

© 1998 Hopscotch Educational Publishing

Written by Frances Mackay
Series design by Blade Communications
Illustrated by Pat Murray
Cover illustration by Susan Hutchison
Printed by Clintplan, Southam

Frances Mackay hereby asserts her moral right to be identified as the author of this work in accordance with the Copyright, Designs and Patents Act, 1988.

ISBN 1-902239-00-8

All rights reserved. This book is sold subject to the condition that it shall not, by way of trade or otherwise, be lent, hired out or otherwise circulated without the publisher's prior consent in any form or binding or cover other than that in which it is published and without a similar condition, including this condition, being imposed upon the subsequent purchaser.

No part of this publication may be reproduced, stored in a retrieval system, or transmitted, in any form or by any means, electronic, mechanical photocopying, recording or otherwise, without the prior permission of the publisher, except where photocopying for educational purposes within the school or other educational establishment that has purchased this book is expressly permitted in the text.

Using Stories
KS2: Y5–6/P6–7

Introduction

ABOUT THE SERIES

Developing Literacy Skills is a series of books aimed at developing key literacy skills using stories, non-fiction, poetry and rhyme, spelling and grammar, from Key Stage 1 (P1–3) through to Key Stage 2 (P4–7).

The series offers a structured approach which provides detailed lesson plans to teach specific literacy skills. A unique feature of the series is the provision of differentiated photocopiable activities aimed at considerably reducing teacher preparation time. Suggestions for using the photocopiable pages as a stimulus for further work in the classroom is provided to ensure maximum use of this resource.

ABOUT THIS BOOK

This book is for teachers of children at Key Stage 2 Y5–6 and Scottish levels P6–7. It aims to:

✦ develop children's literacy skills through exposure to and experience of a wide range of stimulating literature with supporting differentiated activities which are both diversified and challenging;
✦ support teachers by providing practical teaching methods based on whole-class, group, paired and individual teaching;
✦ encourage enjoyment and curiosity as well as developing skills of interpretation and response.

CHAPTER CONTENT

✦ Overall aims

These outline the aims for both lessons set out in each chapter.

✦ Featured books

This lists the books used in the lessons together with story synopses or reasons for using particular texts.

✦ *Intended learning*

This sets out the specific aims for each individual lesson within the chapter.

✦ *Starting point*

This provides ideas for introducing the activity and may include key questions to ask the children.

✦ *Activity*

This explains the task(s) the children will carry out in the lesson without supporting photocopiable activities.

✦ *Using the differentiated activity sheets*

This explains how to use each sheet as well as providing guidance on the type of child who will benefit most from each sheet.

✦ *Plenary session*

This suggests ideas for whole-class sessions to discuss the learning outcomes and follow-up work.

✦ *Using the photocopiable sheets as a stimulus for further work*

This is a useful list of further activities that can be developed from the activity sheets. These ideas maximise the use of the photocopiable pages.

✦ *Other ideas for using . . .*

This contains other ideas for using the genre of books explored in each chapter. The ideas will have completely different learning intentions from the featured lessons and provide a range of alternatives.

And finally . . .

At the end of the book is a list of all the texts used in the chapters so that teachers have access to the publishing details.

Using Stories
KS2: Y5–6/P6–7

Novels

Overall aims

- To analyse the shape and structure of story beginnings.
- To compare openings in several novels.
- To justify ideas, opinions and preferences by reference to texts.

Featured books

Witches
by Roald Dahl
(Use Chapter 1 which uses first person, addresses reader directly, no direct speech, set in England)

The Eighteenth Emergency
by Betsy Byars
(Use Chapter 1 which uses third person, direct speech, set in USA).

Intended learning

- To compare the story openings of different novels.
- To discuss the shape and structure of story beginnings.

Starting point

- Tell the children that you are going to read them two story beginnings. Ask them to listen carefully because they are going to compare the two chapters afterwards. Then, ask the following questions:
- Q Which story beginning did you like the best? Why?
- Q Where do you think the stories were set? What clues tell you this?
- Q What differences did you notice about the way the chapters were written? (Write the differences on the board. Prompt the children if necessary to discuss first and third person, past or present tense, use of direct speech, how the author addresses the reader and so on).
- Q What kind of story do you think each one will be? (genre)

- Q Can you predict what the plot might be? What clues in the text lead you to this conclusion?
- Q Which story beginning do you find the most exciting? Why?
- Q What effect does it create when the author speaks directly to the reader (as in *The Witches*)? Why do you think the author has used this approach?
- Q Do you prefer a short or long story beginning?

Compare these beginnings with other stories. (Byars starts right in the middle of the action, Dahl provides background information first.)

Activities

- Ask the children to select a different novel of their own choice. Make sure the collection includes significant children's authors.
- Divide the children into pairs and ask them to compare the openings of each story by looking at setting, tense, writing style, use of direct speech, story genre and so on.
- Then ask them to select and write out parts of the text they particularly like, such as the opening sentences of a paragraph that they find exciting, good examples of scene setting and so on.
- Finally, ask each person to write which story opening they preferred and say why.

Plenary session

Bring the children together again to share ideas. Ask them to justify or illustrate their ideas and preferences by referring to the text. Do others agree with them? Why did they select these extracts? What makes them 'good' examples? Was it useful to compare different books? How does this help us to develop our understanding of story beginnings? How important do they think the beginning of a novel is – what makes them want to read on? Display the selected extracts and comments about them.

Novels

◆ LESSON TWO ◆

◆ Intended learning

- To write about story beginnings and justify ideas, opinions and preferences by reference to the texts.
- To write own story beginning using ideas and techniques discussed.

◆ Starting point

- Remind the children about the discussions on story beginnings in Lesson 1 by reading out some of their selected extracts and comments from the display. Have they gained any ideas from this discussion that might help them when they write their own stories? What ideas/techniques used in the novels would they like to try out in their own writing? Why? List these ideas so they can refer to it during this lesson. Tell them that they are going to consider two more very short story openings and then they will have the opportunity to try out some of the ideas encountered by writing a story beginning of their own.

◆ Using the differentiated activity sheets

Activity sheet 1

This is aimed at less able children who would welcome a simpler text to read. It uses multiple choice questions and provides structured support for writing the story beginning.

Activity sheet 2

This is aimed at more independent workers who are capable of expressing themselves more confidently in a written format.

Activity sheet 3

This is aimed at more able children who enjoy a more demanding text and would benefit from more challenging questioning.

Throughout the activity, encourage the children to use word banks, dictionaries and thesauruses to collect, build on, edit and revise the words and phrases they use in their writing. Encourage them to refer to the novels they have read and shared to model their own ideas.

◆ Plenary session

Bring the whole class together to share their responses. Discuss which style of story opening they preferred from the two examples given, making sure they support their preferences with reference to the text.

Ask some of them to read out their own story beginning. Ask others to say one good point about it and one thing that might be improved. Discuss words and phrases used and how use of a thesaurus can prevent repetition of over-used words as well as providing a source of good words. Can the others guess how the plot may develop from these beginnings? Share ideas for each piece. Map out what might happen next in several examples.

Let them complete the stories in a follow-up lesson. Encourage them to re-work their story beginnings, building on the knowledge and experience gained from these sessions.

Using Stories
KS2: Y5–6/P6–7

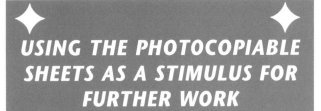

Novels

✦ USING THE PHOTOCOPIABLE SHEETS AS A STIMULUS FOR FURTHER WORK ✦

✦ Cut out the story beginnings of each activity sheet and glue them onto one piece of paper. Photocopy the whole page and use it to make comparisons between the words and phrases used to depict the same story. Which beginning do they prefer out of all six? Why? Which one uses the most descriptive language? Which one gives the reader more information? Which text uses speech which is more realistic? And so on.

✦ Act out the texts with speaking in them (including the children's own beginnings) to help improve the story line and to see how well the dialogue works.

✦ Listening activity – working in pairs, ask one child to read their beginning to the other. Can the partner repeat the story?

✦ Select one child's story beginning. Ask others to finish the story in different ways: humorous, sad, horror, sci-fi, romance and so on. Make a class book with one page for the beginning and different pages for the plot.

✦ Ask the children to write their story beginnings on card for others to choose from to finish the story.

✦ OTHER IDEAS FOR USING NOVELS ✦

✦ Compare story endings – how does the plot build up to its climax? How are the character's problems solved?

✦ Map out the story characters and draw lines showing the relationships between them.

✦ Keep reading journals of books read to note likes/dislikes and reflections.

✦ Re-write a section of a novel and discuss how this might influence the plot.

✦ Investigate the purpose of different characters in the story – good character, bad character, problem-solver and so on.

✦ Map out the story plot by writing a brief summary of each chapter.

✦ Write a new chapter in the same style as the novel.

✦ Use the novel for shared reading to develop an understanding of plot, setting and character by sharing responses.

✦ Explore how the text is used to create atmosphere – compare this with other books.

✦ Investigate narrative structure – how the chapters are linked together and how the passing of time is portrayed.

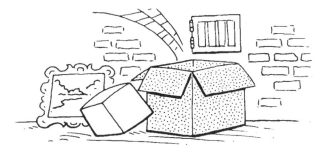

Using Stories
KS2: Y5–6/P6–7

Activity 1   Name _____

◆ Story beginnings ◆

1 Read the following story beginnings and circle your answers.

1
I like living in my village. My family have lived here for a very long time. My parents own the village shop and I work there too. I never thought I would ever leave Scotland but one day a circus came to town and I took up the job of feeding the animals. Now I am looking forward to my first day in a new place.

2
"Look out!" said Peter.
Lloyd jumped out of the way just as a big box came crashing to the floor.
"Now look what you have done. Mum will be very cross," said Peter.
"Don't fuss. Look what was behind the box," said Lloyd.
On the wall they could see a trap door.
"Let's see what's inside," said Lloyd.

◆ The story I liked best was: No. 1   No. 2

◆ I liked it best because: it sounds as if something exciting will happen.

                                   it was easy to read.

◆ I think No. 2 will be: adventure   mystery   horror   fantasy

◆ Which is true?   Both are written in the first person.

                                   One has two characters in it.

2 Now you are going to write your own story beginning. Copy and complete the passage below so that the story sounds exciting. Use a dictionary or thesaurus to help you.

Robert and Emma raced along the path.
"Quick, we'll never get to _____ if you don't hurry," said Emma.
They were soon there and Robert knocked on the door. The door slowly creaked open and there stood _____. She was very_____ and _____. Robert kept looking at her.
"You are the only person we know who can help us," said Emma.
"Help you do what?" _____ replied.
"We must find out how to _____" said Robert.
"Oh dear. Well you must do three things." she replied.

Using Stories   Photocopiable

KS2: Y5–6/P6–7   7

Activity 2   Name _____

◆ Story beginnings ◆

◆ Read the following story beginnings then answer the questions.

1
I was born in a remote village in Scotland. My family have lived in our house for many generations. Very few people in our family have ever left Scotland's shores, not for very long anyway, as they always seem to return here. As for me, I can't wait to get away, not because I dislike the area, but because I want to travel and see the world. That's why I jumped at the chance to join a travelling circus when it came into town. And so, here I am at last on the road to goodness knows where!

2
"Look out!" screamed Peter. "The whole thing's going to fall!"

Lloyd quickly jumped out of the way as a huge box tumbled to the floor.

"I told you to be careful. Now look what you've done. Mum'll go spare."

"Don't worry," said Lloyd. "We'll soon clear it up. But just look what was behind that box!"

Lloyd was pointing to a trap door in the wall. "I wonder what's in there?" he asked.

◆ Underline one line in each passage that lets us know that something exciting is going to happen.

◆ Which passage did you enjoy best? Explain why, referring to the passage.

_____
_____

◆ What kind of story do you think the first one will be? Why do you think this?

_____
_____

◆ Write down two differences in the writing styles between the two passages.

_____

◆ Use the back of this page to write a story beginning of your own. Try to make it sound interesting and exciting. Use a dictionary or thesaurus to help you.

Using Stories   Photocopiable
KS2: Y5–6/P6–7

Activity 3   Name _____

◆ Story beginnings ◆

◆ Read the story beginnings below. Answer the questions. Use the back of this sheet if you need more space.

1

My ancestors have abided here in Scotland for countless generations. Our family has survived times of war, famine and many hardships, but the love we feel for our country remains undiminished. My parents rarely leave the place, except for their annual holidays, and I must admit, I too cherish the tranquility and breathtaking beauty that surround us. No-one then, could have been more surprised than I was myself when I suddenly announced a momentous decision – I had decided to join a circus to see the world! And so here I am about to embark on a wonderful journey. My whole being is quivering with the anticipation of what lies ahead.

2

"Look out!" screamed Peter. "The boxes are collapsing!"

Lloyd deftly darted to one side seconds before several huge boxes crashed to the floor.

"I told you to be careful. Now look what you've done. I'll be grounded for a week when Mum sees this."

"Stop whingeing," retorted Lloyd. "We'll soon clear it up. Just look what was hidden behind those boxes!"

Lloyd was beside himself with excitement. Peter's gaze followed Lloyd's outstretched arm which was frantically pointing to the wall and there his eyes focused on a trap door hitherto unknown to either of them.

◆ Why do you think it was described as a 'momentous' decision to leave Scotland?

_____

◆ How does the author create an atmosphere of excitement in passage No. 2?

_____

_____

_____

◆ Which passage do you prefer? Explain why as fully as you can, referring to the author's choice of words and phrases and the writing style used.

_____

_____

_____

◆ Use the back of this page to write a story beginning of your own. Try to make it sound as interesting and exciting as you can. Use a dictionary or thesaurus to help you.

Using Stories   Photocopiable
KS2: Y5–6/P6–7

Classic fiction

Overall aims

- To explore how the text is used to create characters.
- To explore how language and vocabulary create the style and voice of characters.
- To compare and evaluate the written and television version of the same novel.

Featured book

The Lion, The Witch and The Wardrobe
by C S Lewis

Story synopsis: This book tells the story of four children who are evacuated to the countryside during the war. The youngest, Lucy, finds a way to get into another world called Narnia through a wardrobe in a spare room in the country house. The children meet several animals who tell them about the White Witch who is keen to capture them. With the help of a magical lion called Aslan, the children defeat the witch.

Intended learning

- To explore the language used to describe characters.
- To discuss how the characters might speak and to re-create the style and voice of the characters through role-play.

Starting point

- Read the story to the children before Lesson 1.
- How do they think the author portrayed the characters? What do they imagine Lucy looks like? What clues are there in the story that help us to create this picture? Do we all imagine her to look the same? Ask some of the children to describe Lucy – are their descriptions similar?
- Copy out part of the text (prior to the lesson) which describes the faun (end of Chapter 1) and/or the witch (end of Chapter 3) and provide the children with a copy. Ask them to do a quick drawing using the description as a guide. How good do they think the description is? Did it help them to decide how the character might look? Which parts of the text helped the most? Even with the same description, are the drawings alike or do we interpret the text in different ways? Are we influenced by images of other fauns/witches we have seen in other books, for example?
- What do the children think the characters might sound like? Start with the faun and the witch, then the children and Aslan. What type of voices do they think they might have? Why?
- Read out some of the dialogue from Chapter 1 and ask some of the class to act out the voices – do others agree that this is how they might sound? Discuss the words used by the children such as 'old chap', 'he's an old dear', 'I say let's go explore'. Are these expressions still used today? Do the words help us to build up a picture?

Activity

- Divide the children into four groups and ask them to act out the first chapter from where the children arrive at the house to where Lucy meets the faun. Tell them not to worry about using exact dialogue from the book but to try and re-create the style and voice of the characters and how they might move and behave.

Plenary session

Ask each group to act out part of their play. Have they captured the style and voice of the characters? How convincing are they? Are the characters portrayed in similar ways by each group? Do some characters have dialogue that is particularly memorable from the story? Has this influenced how they think the character might sound and behave? Tell the children that they are to watch a television version of the book to see how their interpretation compares with the film producer's ideas.

Classic fiction

◆ Intended learning

+ To compare and evaluate the written and television versions of the same story.
+ To discuss the reasons for the story's lasting appeal.

◆ Starting point

+ Watch the television version (BBC Family Classics) before this lesson.
+ During the video, ask the children to make notes of all the changes they notice between the book and the television version.
+ After the video, ask the children to look at their drawings of the faun/witch completed in Lesson 1. How do their versions compare with the film's? Why do they think changes were made? Discuss how stories can evoke different images in people's minds and how difficult it is to re-create characters such as animals and witches in films without using animation.
+ Tell the children that they should use their notes when watching the video to make more detailed comparisons between the book and the television version when they carry out the next activity.

◆ Using the differentiated activity sheets

Activity sheet 1

This is aimed at less able writers. The teacher may need to read out the questions for them. It may be beneficial if these children work as a group to share their ideas and to discuss each question in more detail with the teacher.

Activity sheet 2

This is aimed at more independent readers and writers who are capable of making their own judgements about the book and television versions.

Activity sheet 3

This is aimed at more able children. It is less structured and provides more space for more detailed responses.

◆ Plenary session

After the children have completed the tasks, ask them to sit with a partner to share their ideas. Pair up children from different groups. Ask them to choose one or two of their questions to share. Then bring the whole class together to compare their thoughts on how well the television version represented the book. Do they think the producers have made a good attempt at interpreting the story? Ask some of the children to give an example of a change in the television version – is the change a good or bad one? Why do they think this change was made? Do the changes affect the story?

Tell them the book was written in 1950 and yet the television version came out in 1988. Why is it that children of today can still enjoy the story? Ask them to spend five minutes discussing this in pairs and then share their responses.

Using Stories
KS2: Y5–6/P6–7

Classic fiction

USING THE PHOTOCOPIABLE SHEETS AS A STIMULUS FOR FURTHER WORK

- Make character studies – draw and write about a character comparing the book with the television version.

- Write a piece for the newspaper for the television premier of the film.

- Make two lists – why the book is better and why the film is better. Use the lists to set up a class debate.

- Write a book blurb and a video cover blurb summarising the story.

- Pretend to interview the people acting the characters in the film – how did they enjoy playing the part? How closely do they think their part relates to the book? What would they change about their character? Which part of the film did they enjoy doing the best and why?

- Write a letter from the author to the film producer saying what he thought of the television version. Was he happy or not?

- Find out how many children preferred the television version to the book. List their reasons. Can films encourage us to read the book? Can reading the book encourage us to watch the film?

- Set the children a homework task to ask their parents/grandparents what their favourite book was when they were the same age. Why did the adults like that book better than any others? Make a class collection of these titles to encourage the children to share what they found out about them and to invite them to read them.

OTHER IDEAS FOR USING CLASSIC FICTION

- Participate in a shared reading of the story to practise voice characterisation.

- Carry out character studies – follow one character from the beginning to the end – how does the character change throughout the story? How does the author make us feel towards this character? How relevant is this character in today's world?

- Explore unusual language and vocabulary – discuss how expressions and words change in meaning over time.

- Write a modern-day version of the story.

- Write a short section of the story for television with stage directions, script and setting descriptions.

- Storyboard a scene from the story.

- Read the story up to the last chapter. Ask the children to write the last chapter, using the same language and character styles.

Using Stories
KS2: Y5–6/P6–7

Activity 1   Name _____

◆ The Lion, The Witch and The Wardrobe ◆

✦ Compare the book with the television version.

1 Tick the box if you think any of these things were different in the television version compared with the book.

Lucy	☐	The White Witch	☐
Edmund	☐	Mr Tumnus	☐
Peter	☐	Mr and Mrs Beaver	☐
Susan	☐	Aslan	☐
The professor	☐	The professor's house	☐
Mrs Macready	☐	The wardrobe	☐
The dwarf	☐	The witch's castle	☐

2 Questions about the television version. Answer yes or no.

Did the children sound and speak as you thought they would? _____
Were there lots of changes to the story? _____
Was the film a good version of the book? _____
Did you enjoy the film? _____

3 Write down one thing you did not like about the film.

_____

4 Which did you enjoy most – the book or the film? _____
Write down why you liked it best.

_____
_____
_____
_____
_____

Using Stories
KS2: Y5–6/P6–7

Photocopiable

Activity 2　　　　　　　　　　　　　　　　　　　　　Name _____

◆ The Lion, The Witch and The Wardrobe ◆

◆ Compare the book with the television version.

1 Which did you enjoy the most, the book or the film? _____

　Write down your reasons why.

　_____
　_____
　_____
　_____

2 Write down two things the television version changed from the book.

　a _____
　b _____

3 Do you think these changes were good or bad? Write your ideas here:

　_____
　_____
　_____
　_____

4 Were you disappointed with anything in the television version?
　Write down why or why not.

　_____
　_____
　_____
　_____

5 Did the children look and sound as you expected them to in the film? _____

6 Were the settings how you expected them to look in the television version? _____

7 What do you think you should do first – read the book or watch the film?
　Use the back of this sheet to write down your reasons.

Using Stories　　　　　　　　　　　　　　　　　　　　　　　　　Photocopiable
KS2: Y5–6/P6–7

Activity 3 Name _____

◆ The Lion, The Witch and The Wardrobe ◆

◆ Compare the book with the television version.

1 Write down three changes in the film compared with the book.

a _____

b _____

c _____

2 For each of these three changes, write down why you think it was changed for the film and whether you think the change is acceptable.

a _____
   _____
   _____

b _____
   _____
   _____

c _____
   _____
   _____

3 Write down your thoughts about the characters in the film. Did they look, sound and behave as you expected them to? Refer to the book in your answer.

_____
_____
_____
_____
_____

4 Use the back of this sheet to write down which version you enjoyed most – the book or the film. Give your reasons why.

Playscripts

Overall aims

+ To investigate playscript conventions.
+ To investigate how characters are portrayed through dialogue action and description.
+ To produce own playscript.

Featured book

Roald Dahl's *James and the Giant Peach*: A Play
adapted by Richard R George

Synopsis: this book presents Roald Dahl's story in play format. It provides suggestions for staging, costumes, scenery and lighting as well as ideas for using conventional playscript directions throughout the text.

Intended learning

+ To investigate playscript conventions such as stage directions, layout and presentation of dialogue.
+ To investigate how the behaviour and feelings of characters are portrayed through playscript conventions.

Starting point

+ Copy out Scene 1 from the play and make several photocopies before the lesson. Divide the class into groups of seven children and provide them with the copies of Scene 1. Explain that you would like them to look at the way plays are written by studying this well-known story by Roald Dahl. Ask each group to work together in different areas of the classroom to read out the parts of the characters in this first scene of the play. When the groups have completed this task, bring the class together again. Did they have any trouble reading the play? How did they know which parts to say out loud? Do we read out text in brackets? Why not? Why do they think some dialogue is written in capital letters? In what ways is a play different from or the same as a story?

Activity

+ Tell the children they are to work in the same groups to consider how plays are presented in more detail. Ask each group to appoint a scribe to write down their ideas about the following questions, which you could write on the board. They will need to refer to their copies of Scene 1.

Q How different is the layout of the text from that in stories?
Q Why do you think the character's names are written in capital letters each time they speak?
Q How do the characters know what to do and how to speak when the play is acted out?
Q How do we know what kind of characters the people are? What clues are we given?
Q How important is the role of narrator? Why?

Plenary session

Bring the class together again to share their responses to the questions. Discuss how playscripts use conventions such as stage directions to direct the actors. Compare the layout and how paragraphing may differ from conventional stories. Discuss techniques used to portray characters, such as using the narrator to describe them. Discuss how many other people they think might be needed to do the play apart from the characters. How do we know what props are needed and how the stage might look? Explain that many playscripts also provide information on how to perform the play. Show them the ideas in the back of the *James and the Giant Peach* play and read out some of the suggestions.

Playscripts

◆ LESSON TWO ◆

◆ Intended learning

✦ To produce own playscript, showing an understanding of playscript conventions.

◆ Starting point

✦ Remind the children about the discussions in Lesson 1 by asking them to tell you the things playscripts have that make them different from storybooks. Discuss how important it is for plays to have stage directions so that the actors know what to do and how important narrators are so that the audience knows what is happening.
✦ Practise writing stage directions by asking them to think of a well-known traditional tale, such as The Three Bears and suggesting ideas for setting the stage for the first scene. Discuss how this might be written down as well as the words the narrator might use. Remind them about the use of brackets in dialogue which tells the character how to say the lines and how to act the part. Make sure the children understand the basics of playscript conventions before carrying out the next activity.

◆ Using the differentiated activity sheets

Tell them that they are going to have a go at producing their own playscript of another traditional story, Jack and the Beanstalk, and that they will be using activity sheets to guide them. They may work in pairs or individually. Provide copies of playscript texts for them to use as models when completing the tasks.

Activity sheet 1

This is aimed at less able children who would find setting out a playscript difficult but who would benefit from a sequencing activity that shows they understand playscript conventions.

Activity sheet 2

This is aimed at more independent workers who are capable of writing their own script but would benefit from definite guidelines.

Activity sheet 3

This is aimed at more able children who need less structure and guidance.

◆ Plenary session

✦ Bring the class together again. Discuss any problems they may have had. Was the task made easier because they were using a familiar story? Why? Which part of the text was the most difficult to complete (or sequence)? How difficult are stage directions to write? How important are they? Compare the dialogue written by different people. Did everyone stick closely to the original tale? Compare sentences used by different children – which do they think would sound best on stage? Why?
✦ Find time to act out the plays in small groups to see how well they cohere.
✦ The children may wish to write their own Scene 2 for *James and the Giant Peach* at another time (either adhering to the original version or making up their own), thereby reinforcing the skills developed in Lessons 1 and 2.
✦ If a study of a Shakespearean play is appropriate, the series *Shakespeare, the Animated Tales*, abridged by Leon Garfield is accessible to Primary-aged children.

Using Stories
KS2: Y5–6/P6–7

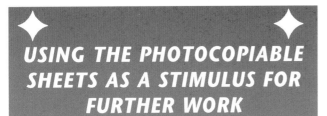

Playscripts

USING THE PHOTOCOPIABLE SHEETS AS A STIMULUS FOR FURTHER WORK

- The children could make a list of props, scenery and costumes they think would be needed, using the playscript text as a guide.

- Change the stories into comedies, horrors or romances and act them out.

- Play *Who Said This?* Read out dialogue from the plays for others to guess who would have said it.

- Role-play a producer being interviewed about the play before opening night – what would he/she say about it?

- Draw costumes/scenery for the play.

- Make a miniature set showing the scenery changes. Use torches for lighting effects. Talk through the changes and effects with a partner.

- Use the plays to make a class picture book with everyone contributing a page.

OTHER IDEAS FOR USING PLAYSCRIPTS

- Dramatise scenes from familiar stories.

- Use playscripts for group reading to practise intonation and characterisation and to discuss conventions.

- Storyboard a scene from a play – how might it look if it had to be filmed?

- Change the characters in plays, such as the strong/harsh people into timid/quiet ones. How might their intonation and dialogue change?

- Re-write parts of stories as plays. Discuss the problems involved and whether the play or the story is more effective.

- Watch theatre or film versions of plays/novels to compare treatments and to discuss preferences.

- Write additional scenes using the same styles and voices of characters.

- Write a comment about the play from different characters' point of view.

- 'Go on location'. Use magazine pictures or real places to find suitable settings for scenes – justify choice.

- Make cartoon strips of scenes, using appropriate dialogue.

Using Stories
KS2: Y5–6/P6–7

Activity 1 Name _____

◆ A playscript ◆

◆ Cut out the boxes below. Put them in order so that the stage directions and dialogue make sense.

MOTHER: We can't just live on milk! You'll have to take the cow to market and get the best price you can.

OLD MAN: Hello boy (lifts his cap). Where are you off to then?

NARRATOR: So Jack took the beans and returned home. When he showed his mother she was hopping mad.

NARRATOR: Jack creeps under the huge castle door. He sees an enormous giant asleep. Next to him is a huge pile of gold coins. Suddenly the giant awakens.

OLD MAN: (laughing) Ha! Call that a cow! You won't get much for that old thing. Here, I'll give you some beans for her.

JACK: Alright mother. I'll take the cow now if you like. (He grabs the cow's leash.)

(Jack is milking the cow. Jack's mother is standing nearby with her hands on her hips.)

JACK: Wow! Look at that huge castle. I wonder who lives there? (He walks towards it).

GIANT: (bellowing) Fee! Fi! Fo! Fum! I smell the blood of an Englishman (peering round). Who is it? Who's there? I'll get you!

JACK: I'm off to market to sell our cow.

(Jack's mother moves off-stage right. Jack walks the cow around the stage. An old man enters stage left).

OLD MAN: Ah, yes. (smiling). But these are MAGIC BEANS. Plant them tonight and see what happens.

JACK: Beans! My mother will kill me if all I bring back home is a handful of beans!

MOTHER: (screams) BEANS! You sold our cow for some stupid beans! Go to bed you silly boy. There'll be no supper for you! (She throws the beans out the window)

NARRATOR: Next morning Jack awoke to find a huge beanstalk growing outside his window. Slowly he climbed right up to the very top.

NARRATOR: But Jack was very quick. He grabbed as many coins as he could carry and climbed back down the beanstalk before the giant realised. When he showed his mother, she was very pleased and the two of them lived happily ever after.

Using Stories   Photocopiable
KS2: Y5–6/P6–7

Activity 2 Name _____

◆ A playscript ◆

◆ Complete this playscript. Think carefully about what happens in the story. Complete the dialogue. Write the stage directions in the brackets.

(Jack is milking the cow. His mother is standing nearby with her hands on her hips.)

MOTHER: We can't just live on milk. You'll have to take the cow to market and get the best price you can.

JACK: _____

(Jack's mother moves off stage right. Jack _____ An old man enters on stage left.)

OLD MAN: Hello boy (_____) Where are you off to then?

JACK: _____

OLD MAN: Ha! You won't get much for that old cow. Here I'll give you these beans for her.

JACK: _____

OLD MAN: These are MAGIC BEANS. Plant them tonight and see what happens.

NARRATOR: So Jack _____

MOTHER: BEANS!! You sold our cow for some stupid beans! (She throws them out the window.)

NARRATOR: Next morning _____
_____

JACK: Wow! Look at that massive castle. I wonder who lives there?
(He _____)

NARRATOR: Jack creeps under the monstrous castle door. He sees an enormous giant asleep. Next to him is a huge pile of gold coins. Suddenly the giant awakes.

◆ Use the back of this page to complete the playscript. Remember to use stage directions as well as dialogue.

Using Stories
KS2: Y5–6/P6–7
Photocopiable

Activity 3 Name _____

◆ A playscript ◆

◆ Complete this playscript. Think carefully about what happens in the story. Complete the dialogue. Write the stage directions in the brackets.

(Jack is milking the cow. His mother is standing nearby with her hands on her hips.)

MOTHER: We can't just live on milk. You'll have to take the cow to market and get the best price you can.

JACK: _____

(_____)

OLD MAN: Hello boy. Where are you off to then?

JACK: _____

OLD MAN: _____
_____

JACK: _____
_____
_____

OLD MAN: _____
_____

NARRATOR: So Jack takes the beans and returns home. When he shows his mother she is very angry.

MOTHER: _____
_____

(She throws the beans out the window.)

NARRATOR: Next morning _____
_____
_____

JACK: Wow! What a huge castle. I wonder who lives there?

NARRATOR: Jack _____
_____
_____

GIANT: _____
_____

◆ Complete your playscript on the back of this sheet. Use stage directions and dialogue.

Fairy tales

 ### Overall aims

+ To identify the common features of fairy tales.
+ To investigate different versions of the same story.

 ### Featured book

Fairy Tales
retold by Rose Impey
Or any such collection of traditional tales (this collection has 15 tales).

LESSON ONE

 ### Intended learning

+ To identify and discuss common themes in fairy tales.

 ### Starting point

+ Ask the children to tell you the names of any Fairy Tales they know. Write the names on the board. Do they have a favourite? Why do they like this one in particular? Can they remember the stories well? When did they first read/listen to them? What age group do they think they are for? Why? Can they suggest why the stories were told in the first place? Do they think they were told orally or in a written form? How would the stories be passed on from one person to another? Explain that most tales were passed on orally and in doing so, each person may have changed the story slightly thus giving rise to different versions of the same tale.
+ Ask the children to tell you if they think the stories in Fairy Tales are similar to each other in any way. Explain that they are going to carry out a task to explore this idea. If necessary, read the children some of the tales from the collection to refresh their memories before carrying out the activities.

 ### Using the differentiated activity sheets

Provide the children with the appropriate activity sheet. Those doing sheets 2 and 3 can work in pairs or individually. The teacher will need to work with the children doing sheet 1.

Activity sheet 1

This is aimed at children who need a lot of teacher support. After they have cut out the sections, ask them to sort them in the following ways:
+ place the pictures under the appropriate character trait (good, bad and so on) headings;
+ match the character illustrations to the story titles;
+ sort the pictures into those characters who have a happy ending and those who don't;
+ match the character traits to each title (do they all have the same traits?);
+ put the story titles in order from the most well-known story to the least (in their opinion).

After each activity, share the results – do they all agree?

Activity sheet 2

This is aimed at more independent readers and writers.

Activity sheet 3

This is aimed at more able children who have a wide experience of fairy tales.

 ### Plenary session

Bring the class together again to share the results of the activities. Make an agreed class list of common features of fairy tales. Discuss why they think the stories were written and what the messages might be. Discuss gender issues – is the brave person always the prince? Is the princess always weak and helpless?

Fairy tales

◆ LESSON TWO ◆

◆ Intended learning

✦ To investigate different versions of the same fairy tale.
✦ To write own modern-day version of a traditional tale.

◆ Featured books

Grimms' Fairy Tales
translated by Peter Carter
Snow White and the Seven Dwarfs
retold by Jenny Koralek
Snow White in New York
by Fiona French

◆ Starting point

✦ After reading the two versions of *Snow White* as retold by Peter Carter and Jenny Koralek, ask the children to tell you all the differences between the two stories. Why do they think some of these changes have been made? What are the similarities between the two stories? Which version do they like best? Why? Which version do they think is the oldest? What clues in the text tell them this?
✦ Next, read the Fiona French story which sets Snow White in modern times. What do they think of this version? Discuss all the references to the older versions, such as the New York Mirror newspaper instead of a mirror on the wall. Ask why they think Snow White was described as 'a poor little rich girl'.
✦ List the things that are essential to the story in all versions – Snow White, step-mother, poison, seven men and so on. Discuss how each item/character was portrayed in the different stories. Which version do the children like best? Can they suggest why, using parts of the story to justify their opinions?

◆ Activity

✦ Ask the children to think of another fairy tale that they know really well. Working in pairs, ask them to write down a list of essential items/characters present in the story and then match this list to modern-day equivalents.
✦ Ask them to use this list to help them write a modern-day version of the story along the lines of *Snow White in New York*. Provide as many copies of fairy tale stories as possible so that the children have readily accessible references should they need them.
✦ If necessary, match up less able writers with more able ones so that the children can concentrate more on developing the story than on coping with writing skills.
✦ Work with each pair in turn while they write their story to ensure the storyline matches the original and that no important parts of the plot have been omitted.

◆ Plenary session

At the end of the session ask some children to read out the beginning of their story. Can the others guess the original tale? What are the good points about these beginnings? Can others make useful suggestions for improvements? Can they predict what might happen next? How easy did they find writing the story? Does it help to have the plot already worked out? How well did they work together? What problems did they have? How did they solve these?

Allow more class time for the children to complete the stories and make them into a class collection or individual story books for the class library.

Using Stories
KS2: Y5–6/P6–7

23

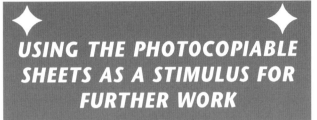

Fairy tales

USING THE PHOTOCOPIABLE SHEETS AS A STIMULUS FOR FURTHER WORK

✦ Cut out the pictures on Activity sheet 1 and write character profiles about them.

✦ Draw fairy tale characters and write sentences and words around them to describe their characters.

✦ Make a display about fairy tales that lists good characters, bad characters and common themes/ideas together with samples of books.

✦ 'What are fairy tales?' – write a piece which describes the kind of stories they are as if telling someone who has never heard of them.

✦ Make fairy-tale wheels, like pie segments, with the names of characters who are good, bad, ugly, beautiful, wise, foolish and so on in each segment.

OTHER IDEAS FOR USING FAIRY TALES

✦ Make up television or radio news reports outlining crimes committed in the tales – act out being a newsreader.

✦ Write stories with characters and plots from lots of different tales or introduce a character from one story into another to change the ending.

✦ Make up recipes, such as 'How to get rid of the wolf' for Little Red Riding Hood.

✦ Write stories by changing the bad character into a good character.

✦ Dramatise the stories as plays or puppet shows.

✦ Play 'Who dunnit?' – give a list of clues to help solve who did the crime, for example silken ribbon, hair comb and apple (Snow White).

✦ Make up a quiz about the stories using the fairy tale books in the classroom for reference.

✦ Write letters to a newspaper complaining about particular goings-on, such as a letter complaining about the houses built by the Three Pigs without planning permission.

✦ Play *Guess the Character* – describe looks, personality, hobbies and so on for others to guess who it is.

✦ Pretend to ring up characters on a phone and act out what they might say to each other.

Using Stories
KS2: Y5–6/P6–7

Activity 1   Name _____

◆ Fairy tales ◆

✦ Cut out each box. Your teacher will tell you what to do next.

Jack and the Beanstalk	Cinderella	Sleeping Beauty
The Three Bears	Hansel and Gretel	Rumpelstiltzskin
Little Red Riding Hood	Beauty and the Beast	Rapunzel

| bad | young | good | old | rich |
| poor | strong | weak | beautiful | ugly |

Using Stories　　　　　　　　　　　　　　　　　　　　　　　　Photocopiable

Activity 2   Name _____

◆ Fairy tales ◆

✦ Write down some common good/kind characters
   found in many fairy tales (for example, a prince).
   _____
   _____

✦ Write down some common bad/evil characters (for example, a witch).
   _____
   _____

✦ What are fairy tale princesses usually like? Describe them.
   _____
   _____

✦ What usually happens to princesses in fairy tales?
   _____
   _____

✦ What usually happens in the end in fairy tales?
   _____

✦ Circle the ideas you think fairy tales are often about:

good and evil   future life   beautiful and ugly people   science fiction

weak and strong people   modern day life   wise and foolish people

magic   happy endings   romance   rich and poor people

✦ Why do you think fairy tales were written for children?
   Is there a message for the reader? Write about this on the
   back of this sheet.

Using Stories   Photocopiable
KS2: Y5–6/P6–7

Activity 3   Name _____

◆ Fairy tales ◆

◆ Write a list of things that are commonly found in fairy tales (for example, castle, magic and prince).
_____
_____

◆ Name some good/kind fairy tale characters.
_____
_____

◆ Name some bad/evil fairy tale characters.
_____
_____

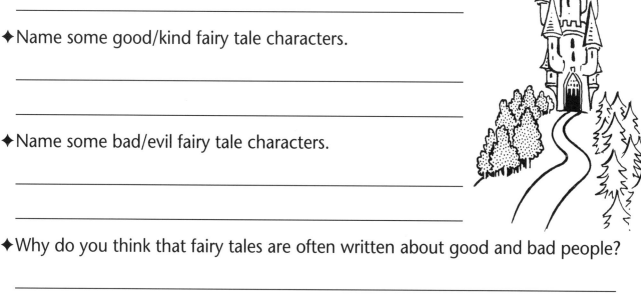

◆ Why do you think that fairy tales are often written about good and bad people?
_____
_____
_____

◆ Most fairy tales have happy endings. Why do you think this might be?
_____
_____
_____

◆ Name some fairy tales with an ugly and a beautiful character in them.
_____
_____
_____

◆ Why do you think fairy tales usually have characters in them who are opposites to each other (such as ugly and beautiful)?
_____
_____
_____

◆ Some people think that fairy tales were written to teach children certain lessons about life and growing up. On the back of this sheet, write your ideas about this – do you agree or disagree? If you agree, what kinds of lessons do you think fairy tales might teach children?

Using Stories   Photocopiable
KS2: Y5–6/P6–7

Fables

Overall aims

+ To identify features of traditional fables.
+ To distinguish between fables and myths and legends.
+ To write own version of a fable.

Featured book

Aesop's Fables
retold by Jacqueline Morley

Book synopsis: The book includes an introduction about Aesop and how the fables originated, a guide to the animal characters in the fables and an index of morals and themes. There are 72 fables.

Intended learning

+ To identify common features of traditional fables.
+ To distinguish between fables and myths and legends.

Starting point

Note: the children will need to have experience of reading or listening to myths and legends before being able to fully participate in this lesson.

+ Ask them what a fable is. Can they remember any? Who originally told these fables? Read 'Who was Aesop?' from the introduction in the collection of fables. Then read some of the more familiar fables such as 'The Tortoise and the Hare' and 'The Fox and the Crow'. Ask the children to say what the stories have in common and list these on the board (short tale, usually about animals, often humorous, has a special message or moral). What do they think a moral is and why do they think these stories may have been told?

+ Next, read out a few other less well-known fables from the book and ask them what they think the moral is. Can some stories have several messages?
+ Explain that before they were written down, fables and other tales, such as myths and legends, were passed on from one generation to another by word of mouth. What might be the differences between fables, myths and legends? Let them use dictionaries to find out definitions. Share some of these definitions. Is it clear what the differences in the terms are? Explain that you would like them to explore this a little further and that you will return to this question at the end of the lesson.

Activity

Divide the class into small groups, each appointing a scribe. Tell them to divide a page into three columns headed: *Fables*, *Myths* and *Legends* and then consider the following aspects of each:

+ How old are the stories? When do you think they may have been told?
+ Where were they usually set?
+ Who/what are the main characters?
+ What are the stories often about?
+ Why do you think the stories were told?
+ Do you think the stories are true?

Explain that there are no particular 'right' answers. People's ideas vary but they should try to come to some sort of group agreement if possible.

Plenary session

Bring the class together to share their responses. Discuss how difficult it is to separate the three types of stories and how the terms can be used interchangeably. Do they think fables are more easily distinguished than myths and legends? Why? Are myths and legends very similar? In what ways? Finally, encourage the children to read more fables, myths and legends to develop their knowledge and understanding further.

Fables

LESSON TWO

Intended learning

♦ To wite a modern-day fable focusing on planning, reviewing and editing to produce the final form.

Starting point

Review the characteristics of fables by asking the children the following questions:

Q Who was a famous fable story teller?
Q What kind of characters are usually in these stories?
Q How long are the stories?
Q How long ago were they written?
Q What is special about them – why were they told?
Q What are the names of some fables?
Q What is the moral behind them?

Provide copies of fables to read and share for 10 minutes to remind them of the structure and format.

Using the differentiated activity sheets

Tell the children that they are now going to have a go at writing a fable themselves using some modern-day morals. Explain that each group will have a different moral to consider and that part of the activity will be to share the fables at the end of the lesson to see if others can work out what the moral of the story was. Explain that they will also be practising how to plan, review and edit their work in order to arrive at a final version.

Activity sheet 1

This is aimed at those children who need a lot of support with reading and writing and who would benefit from a very structured approach.

Activity sheet 2

This is aimed at more independent workers who are able to read with confidence and have a good understanding of basic punctuation.

Activity sheet 3

This is aimed at more able children who can work with little support and guidance.

Plenary session

Bring the class together again. Ask some of the children to read out their fables. Can others guess what the moral of the story might be? Ask the children with the same activity sheet to form a group. For 10 minutes or so, ask them to share the endings – how many different endings were possible to match the same moral?

Bring the whole class together again to share what they found out. What influenced them to write their own particular ending? Did they remember stories they have read? Did they deliberately try to write a strange ending? Do they think the moral message they had to write is a good one for children to be aware of today? What problems did they have when doing the task? How did they solve them? Did the activity sheet help them to plan, review, edit and write in a more structured way? Are they pleased with the final versions? Could any improvements still be made? Make the final versions into a class book for the reading comer.

Using Stories
KS2: Y5–6/P6–7

Fables

USING THE PHOTOCOPIABLE SHEETS AS A STIMULUS FOR FURTHER WORK

✦ Ask the children to use the method of plan, review and edit to write their own fables. Share ideas for further modern-day type morals.

✦ Use Activity sheet 1 as a model for making cartoon strips of well-known or invented fables.

✦ Collaboratively, think of as many different endings as possible for each activity sheet. Make three books with the beginning on the first page and illustrated endings on the other pages.

✦ Use the method to model a whole-class fable before asking the children to write their own.

✦ Turn the fables into plays and act them out.

✦ Act out cross-examining the characters as in a police investigation – to find out why the characters behaved as they did.

✦ Use the characters in the stories to write a collection of fables about the characters experiencing different dilemmas and situations.

✦ Make a book of fables suitable for school situations to help children make decisions about common problems, dangers and so on.

OTHER IDEAS FOR USING FABLES

✦ Rewrite traditional fables with modern-day settings.

✦ Compare different versions of the same fables to identify common features and to justify preferences.

✦ Read myths and legends and condense the stories into a fable.

✦ Design a poster to match a fable, telling people about the moral.

✦ Write letters to characters in fables, telling them what you think of their behaviour!

✦ Read different fables about particular animals. Discuss what character traits they are portrayed as having. Discuss whether these traits match 'real animal' behaviour, for example are foxes sly?

✦ Write different stories with the same moral.

✦ Expand fables into longer picture books for younger children to read.

✦ Write an assembly based on a fable and its moral.

✦ Write 'moral' recipes, such as 'How to avoid being selfish'.

Using Stories
KS2: Y5–6/P6–7

Activity 1   Name _____

✦ Writing a fable ✦

✦ You are going to plan, review and edit this modern-day fable.

Plan: Look at the following fable. Plan what you think the ending should be by drawing and writing in the final box.

Moral: Never trust a stranger

a young rabbit went for a walk	he met a fox he did not know	where are you off to rabbit he asked

im off to visit my friends in haretown said the rabbit	i know the way let me take you there said the fox	

Review: Read through the fable again. Does it make sense? Does your ending match the moral of the story?

Edit: Use a red pen to change anything to improve the story. Write in more interesting words and sentences if you want to. Use a dictionary or thesaurus to help you. Check the punctuation – add in all the capital letters, fullstops, commas and speech marks.

Write: On a new piece of paper, write out the corrected version as your final copy. Give it a title and do a drawing to go with it.

Activity 2 Name _____

◆ Writing a fable ◆

◆ You are going to plan, review and edit this modern day fable.

Plan: Look at the following unfinished fable. Decide how it should end. What does the boy mouse do? What does his mother decide?

Moral: Girls and boys should have equal opportunities.

Title: _____

a mother mouse was busy telling her offspring about their duties the boys will go outside to search for food while the girls stay here with me to help clean up she said the boy mice ran off laughing glad to be outside away from lots of work one boy mouse stayed because he knew he would be very good at storing away the seeds so he asked his mother if he could help i don't think you'll be as good as the girls she said the boy mouse was not put off by this remark he . . .

_____
_____
_____
_____
_____
_____
_____
_____
_____

Review: Read through the fable again. Does it make sense? Does your ending match the moral of the story?

Edit: Use a red pen to change anything to improve the story. Add in better words and sentences if you think this is necessary. Use a dictionary or thesaurus to help you. Check the punctuation – add in all the capital letters, full stops, commas and speech marks. Give the fable a suitable title.

Write: On a new piece of paper, write out the corrected fable as your final copy. Do an illustration to go with it.

Using Stories Photocopiable
KS2: Y5–6/P6–7

Activity 3 Name _____

◆ Writing a fable ◆

◆ You are going to plan, review and edit a modern-day fable. The moral of this fable is: drugs can be harmful.

Plan: Use these questions to plan out the fable:

What kind of animals are in the story? _____
How will it begin? _____
_____

What happens? _____
_____

How does it end? _____
_____

Write: Now use this space to write out your fable:

Review: Read through your fable. Check that it makes sense. Does it make it clear what the moral is?

Edit: Use a red pen to change anything to improve the story, such as using better words and phrases. Use a dictionary or thesaurus to help you. Check your punctuation carefully.

Re-write: Use another piece of paper to write your final copy. Do an illustration to go with it.

Using Stories Photocopiable
KS2: Y5–6/P6–7   33

Stories from different cultures

Overall aims

- To identify and discuss ways of life in a different culture and compare with own experiences.
- To use information books to supplement and extend the information found in the story.

Featured book

A Thief in the Village and Other Stories
by James Berry

Story synopsis: this book contains nine short stories written about everyday life in a Caribbean village. The language used brings alive the atmosphere, culture and setting of the Jamaican children it portrays.

Intended learning

- To identify aspects mentioned in the story which may be different to Britain's culture/way of life.
- To use reference books to extend the information given in the story.

Starting point

- Tell the children that you are going to read them a story from the Caribbean. Do they know where it is? Use an atlas to find it. If some children have visited or have relatives there, tell them that their expertise may come in handy later! Read the fourth story: 'All Other Days Run Into Sunday'.
- Ask the children to tell you anything in the story that they think is different from life in Britain – begin with food and write up names such as plantain, ackee, saltfish, callulu and breadfruits. Do they know what these foods are? Have they seen or eaten them?
- Discuss what they think it might be like in the Caribbean – would the village houses look like ours? Would the people dress the same as us? What would the climate be like? Why were the children so afraid of the white tourists? Why do you think the folklore about the Blackheart Men came about? What does this tell us?
- Explain to the children that they will now have an opportunity to find out the answers to some of these questions by using some reference books about the Caribbean.

Activity

Divide the children into four groups. Provide each group with a collection of books about the Caribbean and ask them to find out about different aspects of Caribbean life, for example:
- group 1 – what crops and vegetation grow there
- group 2 – what the day-to-day home life is like
- group 3 – what jobs are carried out by adults, what the school day is like
- group 4 – what animals live there.

Encourage them to find out the answers to some of the questions asked at the beginning of the lesson to see if their ideas were correct. Ask each person to write down one different fact each with the whole group deciding the most important things to write.

Plenary session

Ask each group to read out their information to the rest of the class with perhaps each child reading out their own contribution.

- How did they decide which facts were the most important to write down?
- Is life in the Caribbean what they expected?
- How different is it from life here in Britain?

Make a class list of things the same/different between Britain and the Caribbean. Use this information as well as drawing pictures from the books to make a display about life there.

Stories from different cultures

◆ LESSON TWO ◆

◆ Intended learning

+ To compare life in the Caribbean with own experiences.

◆ Starting point

+ Remind the children of the story by James Berry. Go through the story and write up all the things that are special on a Sunday – how Sunday means no jobs to do (carrying water and cutting wood), no school, wearing best clothes to church, special breakfast and Sunday dinner, washing the horses and mules in the sea, resting after dinner, visiting relatives.
+ Tell the children what you like best about Sundays yourself and then ask them to tell you what they think of Sundays – do they look forward to them like the boy in the story? Why/why not? Write up some of the things they like about Sundays.
+ Tell them you would like them to now compare their own lives here in Britain with the lives of the people in the story set in the Caribbean to see what the similarities and differences are.

◆ Using the differentiated activity sheets

Activity sheet 1

This is aimed at those children who need more support. The teacher may need to help the children read the questions and scribe the answers.

Activity sheet 2

This is aimed at more independent readers and writers.

Activity sheet 3

This is aimed at more able children who can reflect on the story to compare it with their own lives.

◆ Plenary session

After the children have completed the sheets, bring the whole class together to share their responses. Discuss each aspect – the chores, the food and the things that happen on Sundays in the two countries.

How different is life for children in the Caribbean compared to most people's lives here? What things are very similar ? Ask them to tell you which country they would prefer to live in and say why.

Have they enjoyed learning about how other people live? Has the story made them want to visit the Caribbean? Has it changed their ideas about what they thought life might be like there? Would they like to find out more about how people live there? Read more stories from the James Berry book and make a class collection of other stories written about Caribbean life.

Using Stories
KS2: Y5–6/P6–7

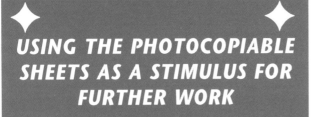

Stories from different cultures

USING THE PHOTOCOPIABLE SHEETS AS A STIMULUS FOR FURTHER WORK

- Make up picture books showing Sunday life in the Caribbean and ones showing Sunday life in Britain.

- Make a Caribbean and a British breakfast menu, illustrating the foods.

- Write a diary of the Caribbean boy's Sunday and then write own diary to compare.

- Write cartoon strips of the Caribbean boy's day, together with British versions.

- Make up a 'photo album' of drawings and writing about the Sunday events.

- Use the feelings expressed in the book and the children's own writing to write poems about Sundays.

- Make a class book with a picture and writing from each child entitled 'The Best Thing about Sunday is . . .'

- Draw a Caribbean postcard and write about what you did on the Sunday you 'visited' there.

- Find out about Caribbean recipes and write a recipe book of Sunday lunches.

- Write about 'The Best Sunday I Ever Had'.

OTHER IDEAS FOR USING STORIES FROM DIFFERENT CULTURES

- Ask people from a variety of cultures to read or tell stories from their own traditions to share first-hand knowledge and experiences.

- Make a display of books with stories from around the world, showing the location of the stories on a map together with any reference books and artefacts.

- Write descriptions of food, clothing or home life using stories as references.

- Make up plays of home life from different countries.

- Write a letter to a character in the book, pretending to be a pen friend.

- Compare myths and legends from different cultures. What are the differences and similarities?

- Compare creation stories from different traditions, dramatise them.

- Study how accents and local dialects are represented in the story. Discuss its purpose in creating atmosphere and authenticity.

- Write a dictionary of words and terms used in the stories to provide a guide for readers.

- Use the stories to write travel brochures or travel guides to the places mentioned.

Activity 1 Name _____

Sundays

◆ Tick the things in the story *All Other Days Run into Sunday* that you also do on Sundays.

wake up early ☐   feed animals ☐   eat a big breakfast ☐

get dressed up ☐   have haircut ☐   wash horse and mule ☐

go to church ☐   eat a big lunch ☐   visit relatives ☐

◆ Compare your life with the Caribbean boy.

On Sundays, the boy's chores are feeding the hens, washing the horse and clearing up the breakfast things.

What chores do you do on Sundays? _____

_____

For breakfast, the boy eats fried fish, fried liver, ackee and saltfish in coconut gravy, callulu, fried plantain, johnny cakes, roast breadfruit, bread and hot chocolate or coffee.

What do you usually eat for breakfast on Sundays?

_____

The boy's family own the following animals — horse, mule, hens, goat and cow.

What animals do you have at home? _____

The best things the Caribbean boy likes about Sundays are: dressing up, having less chores to do, no school, eating a special breakfast and having a three o'clock lunch of beef stew with rice and peas.

What do you like best about Sundays? _____

_____

Using Stories   Photocopiable
KS2: Y5–6/P6–7

Activity 2   Name _____

◆ Sundays ◆

◆ Compare your life with the Caribbean boy from the story *All Other Days Run into Sundays*.

Look at the list of things the Caribbean boy does on Sundays and then write a list of the things you do.

Caribbean boy	Me
wake up early	
feed the hens	
wash the horse	
eat big breakfast	
clear away breakfast things	
cut each other's hair	
get dressed up	
go to church	
eat lunch at 3 o'clock	
have an afternoon nap	
visit relatives	

During the week the boy has to carry water and chop wood. On Sundays he feeds the hens, washes the horse and clears away the breakfast things. Would you enjoy these chores? Why/why not?

_____

What chores do you do?

_____

The boy's family eat a big breakfast together in the sitting room on Sundays. Name some of the foods they eat.

_____

What food do you have for breakfast on Sundays? _____

What does the boy like best about Sundays? _____

What do you like best about Sundays? _____

Using Stories   Photocopiable

Activity 3   Name _____

Sundays

✦ Compare your life with the Caribbean boy from the story
All Other Days Run into Sunday.

The boy in this story describes Sunday as having a special feeling to it which makes it the best day of the week.

Write why the boy liked Sundays so much.

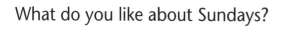

_____
_____

What do you like about Sundays?
_____
_____

Compare the food the boy eats with what you eat on Sundays.
_____
_____

What kinds of things does the boy do on Sundays?
_____
_____

What do you usually do on Sundays?
_____
_____

Where would you rather be on Sundays – here or in the Caribbean?
Give your reasons, referring to your own life as well as that of the Caribbean boy.
_____
_____
_____

Using Stories   Photocopiable
KS2: Y5–6/P6–7

Stories of different genres

Overall aims

- To compare and identify characteristics of different genre.
- To use an anthology of extracts from different genre to identify and justify preferences.
- To use different genre as models to write short passages using appropriate conventions.

Featured books

Smith by Leon Garfield (historical); **Goosebumps: The Curse of the Mummy's Tomb** by R L Stine (horror); **Elephants Don't Sit on Cars** by David Henry Wilson (humorous); **Esio Trot** by Roald Dahl (romance).

Intended learning

- To identify and compare the characteristics of different genre.
- To justify preferences for different genre.

Starting point

- Show the children some novels from a wide range of genre, including some familiar ones. Beginning with the familiar ones, ask them what category the book might be grouped under in a library – horror, romance and so on. With unfamiliar ones, ask them to make a good guess by looking at the cover design, title and author and then by reading the back cover. Read a short extract to try and confirm the category.
- List all the categories on the board. Taking one, perhaps horror as this may be the easiest to consider, ask them to tell you things that are common to horror stories. What kind of characters are usually in them? Where are they often set? What kind of plot is there? What usually happens? What type of language/dialogue is used? Read an extract from *The Curse of the Mummy's Tomb* (Chapter 14 is particularly appropriate) to see if it has the agreed common ingredients of a horror story.

Activity

Working in groups, ask the children to consider the characteristics of other types of stories. Provide the following books:

1. *Smith* – first page of Chapter 1.
2. *Elephants Don't Sit on Cars* – first two pages of Chapter 1.
3. *Esio Trot* – last three pages of book, not including the PS at the end.

Each group should first agree on which category of story they think the extract is. Then ask them to write down all the things they think these kind of stories often have in common in relation to: the types of characters, setting and plot.

Plenary session

Bring the class together again. Read each extract out in turn to compare the conclusions made by the group who had the particular extract with others in the class. What category do they think it is? What common features do these stories have? Write an agreed list of common features for each genre. Which kind of story do the children prefer? Why? Ask for the names of other books which fit the categories. Make collections of books of particular genres. Encourage the children to add to it by bringing books from home. (Vet them for age and content suitability.)

Stories of different genres

◆ LESSON TWO ◆

◆ Intended learning

✦ To write a short passage in the same style as particular genres.

◆ Starting point

✦ Remind the children about the discussion on story genre in Lesson 1. Ask them to recall the names of the different categories. Briefly revise the types of characters, setting and plots common to one or two of the genres. Explain that the writing styles used in each genre is often very different. Refer to the discussion about horror stories and explain that authors of these books often use very short sentences to create an atmosphere of tension and suspense. Read some examples from books that illustrate this.

✦ Ask the children to sit in pairs for five or ten minutes to share ideas about the things that might be common to the writing styles of other genres, such as sci-fi or historical stories. Then tell them that they are to explore their ideas further by doing the next task which involves deciding what genre a piece of writing might be and then writing a paragraph in a particular style. Provide examples of books of different genre and encourage them to refer to them throughout the task.

◆ Using the differentiated activity sheets

Provide the children with the appropriate sheet and explain the task to them. Remind them to use the most descriptive words and phrases they can think of. Encourage them to use dictionaries and thesauruses to help them find the most suitable words.

Activity sheet 1

This is aimed at those children who need more practise at identifying genre and would welcome a shorter writing task. They may need to have the extracts read to them.

Activity sheet 2

This is aimed at more independent workers who are capable of using the conventions and style of particular genre.

Activity sheet 3

This is aimed at more able children as it requires them to identify a greater variety of styles and has a more difficult writing task.

◆ Plenary session

When the children have completed the sheets, bring the class together to share the results. Read out some of the passages and ask different children to read out how they completed them. Does everyone agree on the genre? Are the completed sentences appropriate to the genre? If not, brainstorm some ideas to improve the writing. Which type do the children find easier to write? Can they say why? Is this influenced by their reading experiences? Do you need to read a lot of books in a particular genre before you can write in that style? Which genre(s) may need more research on the author's part to ensure the writing is accurate? Why?

Using Stories

KS2: Y5–6/P6–7

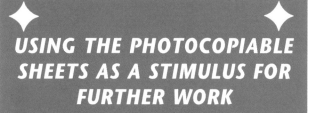
Stories of different genres

USING THE PHOTOCOPIABLE SHEETS AS A STIMULUS FOR FURTHER WORK

- Ask the children to continue one of the passages from the page and make it into a story.

- Use the passages in the boxes on Activity sheet 1 to make picture books by adding to the story beginning.

- Find passages in other books that match these genres to compare how the authors have used characters, language and plot.

- Select one of the passages from the page and write down why you like this style of writing, why you enjoy reading these kinds of books.

- Have fun mixing up different genres in the same story! Can you make all the passages on the page into one story?

OTHER IDEAS FOR USING STORIES OF DIFFERENT GENRES

- Write and draw about typical characters found in particular genres.

- Write book reviews that compare books of the same genre, using examples from the text to illustrate points and justify views.

- Divide the reading corner into particular genre categories. Encourage the children to add to the collections as they read throughout the year to build up stocks.

- Write critical pieces about particular genres – does the book successfully create the atmosphere it intends to? Could this book really be classified as horror? And so on.

- Compare historical books written about the same period in time – how similar/different are they? How accurate is the historical detail? How much knowledge of the period is needed to understand the story?

- Make up phrases/dialogue to act out – others guess what kind of book it might be found in.

- Write about authors who write in specific genres, comparing their books, their success at representing the genre and so on.

- Have a genre of the week or month where you draw the children's attention to authors and titles to widen their knowledge and reading experiences.

Activity 1 Name _____

◆ Writing styles ◆

◆ Cut out the boxes below. Match the pieces of writing that you think go together. There will be one piece of writing left over. In the empty box write some more sentences in the same style to match this one.

John froze to the spot. There was the sound again. What was it? He quickly turned round but saw nothing. His whole body started to tremble and shake. "Run," he thought, "I've got to run."

The Spitfires droned overhead. Billy ran inside to tell his mum. "Quickly, under the table," she said. They could hear the 'ack, ack' of the machine gunners as they tried to hit the German planes. Suddenly there was a deafening thud.

[empty box]

The light was getting brighter and brighter. We had to shield our eyes it was so bright. We heard a whirring noise and felt a rush of wind. The spaceship had landed! Slowly a huge door opened.

The ceiling had collapsed around them. "Are you alright?" asked Billy's mum. "I think so," he spluttered. "We'll be fine, don't worry, the worst's over now. The all-clear siren's just gone."

He ran and ran until his sides began to ache. He dropped down exhausted against an old tree. "Phew, it's gone," he sighed and began to relax. Suddenly, two hands grabbed him by the throat. "Oh no!" he cried.

Using Stories KS2: Y5–6/P6–7 Developing Literacy Skills Photocopiable 43

Activity 2 Name _____

◆ Writing styles ◆

◆ Read the following pieces of writing. Continue each of them in the same style for a few sentences.

The mummy lurched slowly towards them, its arms outstretched. We stood stock-still, frozen with fear. Suddenly . . .

_____
_____
_____
_____

And then he saw it. The tail of the German Heinkel bomber that had crashed into the house next door. He quickly clambered over the pile of debris to see what he could find. There, still all shiny and black was . . .

_____
_____
_____
_____

We watched the bright light skidding across the sky. Then it appeared to grow larger and much brighter. It turned and headed straight for us, causing a huge gust of wind to stir up all the leaves and dust. When we had blinked away the grit from our eyes we couldn't believe what we saw!

_____
_____
_____
_____

Activity 3   Name _____

Writing styles

✦ Read the following passages. Decide which writing style (genre) you think each one is and write your answer in the space provided. Make your choice of genre from the ones in the box.

The Crankzoidian craft landed with a jolt. The Crankzoids alighted to meet our captain. _____

There were two hundred longships in all, some with the black banner of the Khan floating in the breeze. Soon the city walls came into sight and there could be seen the soldiers, their blades glinting in the sun.
_____

My heart skips a beat every time I think of him. I wonder when I will see him again. _____

The mystical music flowed over the glade fairies below. With a wave of his hand, Vallum transformed the grass into shimmering gem stones. _____

horror
science-fiction
romance
historical
humorous
mystery
adventure
fantasy
thriller

✦ Now select a genre from the box that is not represented in the passages above and write a paragraph in this writing style. Try to make the writing specific enough so that other people can identify the genre you have used.

_____
_____
_____
_____
_____

Using Stories   Photocopiable
KS2: Y5–6/P6–7

Comparative stories

Overall aims

+ To compare similarities and differences between books on the same theme written by different authors.
+ To write a comparative essay.

Featured books

The Bully
by Jan Needle
The Angel of Nitshill Road
by Anne Fine

Stories synopses: Both these stories deal with the issues of bullying. The first provides a hard-hitting tale which provokes the reader into considering his own prejudices towards others while the second is a more light-hearted, yet equally pertinent approach.

Intended learning

+ To discuss how the theme of bullying is treated by two different authors.
+ To comment on extracts from texts that show similarities and differences on the way the theme is treated.

Starting point

Read the two stories to the class, then ask:

Q Which story do you prefer? Why?
Q Which book best describes how it feels to be bullied? Can you say why?
Q Why do you think the people being bullied in both stories were reluctant to tell someone about it? Is their reaction a realistic one?
Q Which story would you recommend for younger/older children? Why?
Q Which story ending did you prefer? Why?

Q How is the bully treated differently in the stories?
Q Who do you feel sorry for in each story? Why?
Q What did the stories tell us about how adults can behave towards bullying?
Q Which has the most impact – a lighthearted story like *The Angel of Nitshill Road* or a serious tale like *The Bully*? Why?
Q Which would you recommend to someone who is being bullied? Why?

Using the differentiated activity sheets

Tell the children you would like them to compare the two stories in more detail. The sheets consider three different questions but require a similar task. Thus, a class discussion at the end of the session can focus on nine separate issues from the stories.

Activity sheet 1

This is aimed at less able children. The teacher may need to sit with this group to help read out the questions and scribe any responses if necessary.

Activity sheet 2

This is aimed at more independent children who are able to write their own comments about the two stories.

Activity sheet 3

This is aimed at more able children as the questions are more challenging and require more careful consideration.

Plenary session

After the children have completed the sheets, bring the class together again. Discuss all nine questions by asking someone to respond to each one. Help them to respond to both stories by directing them to consider the two authors. Ask them to sum up by saying how they think the stories have affected their own ideas and approaches to the problems of bullying.

Comparative stories

LESSON TWO

Intended learning

+ To write a comparative essay.

Starting point

+ Remind thd children about the discussions carried out in Lesson 1. Tell them you would like them to have the opportunity to express their opinions about the books in more detail by writing about them. Explain that you would like them to write about how the two authors presented their ideas about bullying. How similar were the books? How different were they? Tell them that they'll begin by planning out what they might say.

Activities

+ Divide the children into mixed ability groups and ask them to appoint a group scribe. Encourage them to use dictionaries, word banks and thesauruses during the activity. Give them the following tasks:
1: Write an opening paragraph which explains what the essay will be about and the authors and titles to be compared.

2: Make a list of things in the stories which are similarly presented and a list of those things that are different.

+ After about 15 minutes, bring the class together again. Share their ideas about an opening paragraph. Write up an agreed 'good' beginning to share the types of words and phrases.

+ Now write up the lists of things that are the same and different about the stories. Choose one from the list and expand on how this might be written in the essay. Write a paragraph on the board as an example. Discuss the idea of using quotes or examples from the books to justify or illustrate a point.

+ Next, ask the children individually to write down a paragraph which states which author they think has written the best book about bullying and say why. After 10 minutes, share some of the ideas. Remind them that there is no 'right' answer to this question and that we all might have very different opinions. Use this time to suggest ways that their ideas can be expressed in words – good phrases to include and so on.

+ Then ask the children to spend about 20 minutes writing their essay, using ideas and suggestions from the discussions about the opening paragraph, things to compare and how they might end the writing.

Plenary session

Bring the class together again and explain that more class time will be given in order to complete the task if necessary, but for the moment, ask the children to work in pairs to help each other edit and re-draft their writing so far. Remind the children to encourage the good things about their partner's work as well as suggesting things to improve. Finally, discuss how they might present a final copy of the essay – things to consider are: use of paragraphing, correct punctuation and spelling as well as neat handwriting or word processing.

Using Stories
KS2: Y5–6/P6–7

Comparative stories

USING THE PHOTOCOPIABLE SHEETS AS A STIMULUS FOR FURTHER WORK

- Carry out a debate on bullying with one side arguing that it's best not to tell anyone and the other side arguing that you should tell.

- Use the books to find other quotes from the stories which could be used to illustrate each question.

- Use the children's responses to make a class book about what to do about bullying.

- Draw pictures of the bullies in the two stories – write sentences about each one, using extracts from the books. Put them under the headings – *A Typical Bully* and *The Unexpected Bully*.

OTHER IDEAS FOR USING COMPARATIVE STORIES

- Make book lists of stories with common themes to display in the class and school libraries. Encourage the children to add to the lists as they read their books.

- Suggest to the children good books to read on particular subjects weekly or monthly – make and share a collection of the books.

- Read two books and ask the children to write a different ending – what should have happened!

- Compare the books by considering fact and opinion – could the events really happen? How realistic is the author's portrayal?

- Write a book critic's review comparing the titles.

- Make advertisement posters – with pictures and a summary of each book showing how different the stories are.

- Write to the authors to ask them why they wrote on the theme – compare answers.

- Write letters to the characters with ideas/ suggestions of what to do using references to other stories on the same issue.

- Make class books on the theme with the children's own ideas and drawings as well as author information and book extracts from stories.

- Make the stories into plays to compare events and outcomes.

Activity 1 Name _____

◆ Comparing stories ◆

◆ Compare two stories about bullying – *The Bully* and *The Angel of Nitshill Road*.

Who do bullies pick on?

"Mark was small for his age. He had strange sticky-up hair and he wore glasses as thick as bottle-ends." (from *The Angel*)

"He did fall over a lot . . . He was slow at reading too. And writing, and arithmetic." (from *The Bully*).

◆ What do you think the authors are trying to tell us? (tick your answer)

Bullies pick on people who are:
different   clever   brave

◆ What do you think the stories tell us about bullying? Put a tick.
1. Not very many people get bullied.
2. Lots of people get bullied for different reasons.

What kinds of things do bullies do?

"Mark the Martian!" he'd call.

". . . he gave Mark's hand a twist-burn."

". . . Barry took Mark's pencil box and hid it . . ." (from *The Angel*).

"She danced up to him and punched him in the face." (from *The Bully*).

◆ Circle the kinds of things the bullies did in these story extracts:

tell tales   call names

punch people   hide things

write nasty notes   trip people

What can you do if you get bullied?

In *The Angel*, the people who were bullied did these things:

"Celeste wrote it down . . . everything that happened."

"Ignore him." ". . . I bit him." "I'll tell her (teacher) all the things you did . . ."

In *The Bully*, Simon tries to fight back and doesn't tell anyone he's being bullied.

◆ On the back of this sheet, write which story you think has the right answers and why.

Using Stories
KS2: Y5–6/P6–7

Photocopiable

49

Activity 2 Name _____

◆ Comparing stories ◆

◆ Compare two stories about bullying – *The Bully* and *The Angel of Nitshill Road*.

How does it feel to be bullied?

" . . . as the hands of the clock rolled round towards playtime, she'd get a horrible feeling, as if her stomach was being gripped by a hard, invisible hand." (from *The Angel*).

" . . . he wanted to fall into her (his mother's) arms and sob his heart out." (from *The Bully*).

◆ Comment on these extracts. Do the two people being bullied show similar feelings? Do you think this is true to life?
_____
_____
_____

◆ How do you think you might feel if you were bullied?
_____
_____
_____

How do the people being bullied react?

" . . . she was forcing back hot tears of embarrassment and shame. And . . . she'd never dare say anything about Barry Hunter to someone she didn't know in case it got back to him and made him worse." (from *The Angel*).

"He was red in the face with anger, his face was ugly and contorted. He was standing with his back to a wall, a large flint boulder in his hand drawn back for hurling." (from *The Bully*).

◆ These extracts show two different ways people react to being bullied. Comment on the way the authors have described their reactions.
_____
_____
_____
_____

Why don't people who are bullied want to tell others?

"Mark brings a lot of it on himself. He has to learn a bit of self-control. They'll have to sort it out themselves." (from *The Angel*).

" . . . there was plenty that he might have said. But instead of saying it . . . Simon took the easy way out." (from *The Bully*).

◆ On the back of this sheet write why you think people are reluctant to admit to being bullied.

Using Stories
KS2: Y5–6/P6–7

Photocopiable

Activity 3 Name _____

◆ Comparing stories ◆

◆ Compare two stories about bullying – *The Bully* and *The Angel of Nitshill Road*.

◆ **What kind of people are bullies?**
Compare the bullies in the two stories (Barry from *The Angel* and Anna and Rebekka from *The Bully*). Which story do you think describes a 'typical' bully? Explain why.

_____
_____
_____
_____

◆ **How do teachers react to bullying?**

" . . . he'd known (the teacher) everything he needed all along. But just like Marigold he had pretended not to see, not to hear, not to understand." (from *The Angel*).

"He needs a short sharp shock . . ." (Mr Kershaw). "I'm giving him the benefit of the doubt . . . I'm going to see if he'll respond to kindness." (Miss Shaw). "This is bullying . . . And I am going to stamp it out." (Mrs Stacey). (from *The Bully*).

◆ Which teacher do you think reacted best to the problems of bullying? Say why you think this, using examples from the story.

_____
_____
_____
_____
_____
_____

◆ **Can the problem of bullying be solved?** Comment on this extract from *The Bully*:

"What would you have done? . . . Kicked them out? So they could go and bully weaklings at another school? Kicked Simon out, so that he could go on being battered without you having to think about it? . . . The truth is, it's a vicious circle. Simon's the sort of kid who's going to attract bullies wherever he goes, but it suits us to deny it . . . So what's the answer? . . . Is there an answer?"

◆ Is there an answer to bullying? Is the solution in *The Angel* story the best? Or is it important to "...make everybody recognise that even kids like Simon have their worth." (as Miss Shaw says in *The Bully*). In the space below and on the back of this sheet, give your opinion about how to solve bullying. Support your ideas by referring to the stories.

_____
_____
_____
_____

Using Stories   Photocopiable
KS2: Y5–6/P6–7

Character studies

Overall aims

- To write a character study.
- To explore how characters are treated by authors.
- To investigate point of view.

Featured book

The Turbulent Term of Tyke Tiler
by Gene Kemp

Story synopsis: This book tells of the trouble Tyke and Danny get into during their last term at Cricklepit Combined School. It outlines the close friendship between them and how Tyke protects Danny because he comes from a poor home background and has speech and learning difficulties. It is an interesting book because it is not until the very end that you learn that Tyke is actually a girl, turning the book into an interesting discussion point about character portrayal.

Intended learning

- To write a character study.
- To explore how characters are treated by an author.

Starting point

- Before the lesson, read the story up until the end of Chapter 14 where it reads: 'only, at that moment, Mrs Somers came round the corner, stopped, spoke to Sir, looked up, saw me and shouted, her face red and corrugated.'
- Ask the children to predict what they think happens next. Do they think Tyke will get out of this unscathed? Discuss the term 'tyke' and why they think Tyke earned this nick-name.

- Explain that before you finish the story you would like them to think more carefully about Tyke's personality to see if that will help us predict what might happen in the end.

Using the differentiated activity sheets

Activity sheet 1

This is aimed at children who will benefit from using a supplied word bank.

Activity sheet 2

This is aimed at more independent children who are able to write their own opinions.

Activity sheet 3

This is aimed at more able children who have the ability to comment on character statements presented in the story and can compare these with their own opinions about the character.

Plenary session

Bring the class together again. Ask them to give their opinions about Tyke. How has the author presented the character – as a hero? A villain? A trouble-maker? Do they feel sympathy towards Tyke? Why? Why does Tyke feel so protective towards Danny? Have Tyke and Danny behaved well or badly? Why?

Return to the story ending. Have they changed their minds about how it might end? Do they think the author wants a happy ending? Read the ending. Were they surprised that Tyke was a girl? What made them think Tyke was a boy? What sort of writing techniques were used to mislead us? Has this changed their opinions about Tyke in any way? Discuss stereo-typing of gender – is it usually boys who get into trouble? Are girls more protective towards their friends than boys?

Using Stories
KS2: Y5–6/P6–7

Character studies

◆ LESSON TWO ◆

◆ Intended learning

+ To investigate point of view.
+ To discuss how the story and characters might look from other character's point of view.

◆ Starting point

+ Remind the children about the character study made on Tyke Tiler in Lesson 1 and how our perception of the character was manipulated by the author. Who do they think is telling the story? How do they know this? Does the postscript offer any clues as to why the story was told in the first place? How might the story change if it was told by a different character? Tell them that they are to explore this further in groups by concentrating on the character of Danny instead of Tyke.

◆ Activity

+ Divide the children into small groups to carry out the same task. Write the following questions on the board (or on paper to photocopy for each group) and ask the groups to pretend that Danny is being interviewed. The group have to decide on the answers they think Danny would give to the questions.

Q Why is Tyke your best friend? How does she help you?
Q Why did you steal the ten pound note?
Q Why did you ask Tyke to hide the money and then put it back. Why didn't you do it yourself?
Q Why didn't you own up about the mouse before Tyke was called to the office?
Q Why did Miss Bonn stick up for you when she found out you'd stolen her money?
Q Why didn't you get the skeleton yourself?
Q How did you feel when Tyke fell back into the stinky water?
Q Did you enjoy learning for the test? Why do you think Tyke made you do this?
Q What did Miss Honeywell say to you that changed you? Why?
Q What happened to you at school when Tyke was away sick?
Q Why did you hide in the old mill even though you hated it?
Q What did you think of Tyke climbing the bell tower?
Q Did you enjoy your last term at school?

◆ Plenary session

Bring the class together again. Share the answers by asking someone from each group to take it in turns to pretend to be Danny and answer the question(s). How similar are the responses? Do we perceive Danny in the same way? Does the author make us feel sympathetic towards Danny in the story? Did this have an effect on the responses to the questions? How different would the story be if it was told by Danny?

Finally, ask the children to consider if they ever think about another character's point of view when reading stories. Do they find it difficult to see the other side of an event/story? Does this relate to our everyday lives? Are there always two sides to a story? Should we try to see other people's point of view when settling arguments, for example?

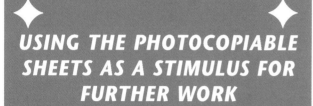

Character studies

USING THE PHOTOCOPIABLE SHEETS AS A STIMULUS FOR FURTHER WORK

- Make up a 'photo album' of Tyke's adventures – draw 'photos' and write sentences underneath.

- Make up wanted posters of Tyke with sentences saying what crimes have been committed, who wants her and what the punishments might be.

- Make up a school report for Tyke. What might Mr Merchant say?

- Hot seating. One person pretends to be Tyke and the others ask questions about her motives, behaviour, relationship with Danny and so on.

- Write about 'My Friend Tyke', as if written by Danny.

- Draw pictures of what you think Tyke looks like and write a description of her underneath.

- Write a letter from Tyke to the Headmaster saying why she had to ring the bell.

OTHER IDEAS FOR USING CHARACTER STUDIES

- Compare character's experiences with own, write down what you would do in the same situation.

- Sort characters into types – happy characters, sad, mean, strong, weak, brave, funny, weird and so on. Make posters of the groupings to display in the book corner.

- Discuss how characters change throughout the story, giving reasons why.

- Write about favourite book characters giving reasons why you like them best.

- Rewrite stories by changing a character with another from a different story.

- Record the character's adventures like a diary expressing the character's feelings and plans.

- Map out the character's traits by listing the events and the consequences like a time line.

- Act out characters from books for others to guess who you are.

- Write stories which follow-up the story using the same characters and settings.

- Make up character passports with 'photo' and personal details.

Using Stories
KS2: Y5–6/P6–7

Activity 1   Name _____

Tyke Tiler

✦ Use words from the box to complete these sentences about Tyke Tiler.

Tyke Tyler is a _____ who goes to Cricklepit Combined School.

Tyke is _____ years old.

Tyke is the _____ child in the Tiler family.

Tyke's _____ is called Danny.

Tyke gets into a lot of _____ at school.

Tyke's favourite teacher is _____.

Tyke looks after Danny because Danny is not very _____.

Tyke helped Danny with the test so they could go to _____ Secondary School.

The Headmaster didn't think Tyke told _____.

Tyke climbed the tower to _____.

| boy
| girl
|
| nine
| eleven
|
| eldest
| youngest
|
| friend
| dog
|
| trouble
| fun
|
| Mrs Somers
| Mr Merchant
|
| bright
| happy
|
| the same
| a different
|
| the truth
| lies
|
| show off
| ring the bell

✦ Now write down some sentences about Tyke. What kind of person is Tyke?

_____
_____
_____
_____
_____

Using Stories   Photocopiable
KS2: Y5–6/P6–7   55

Activity 2 Name _____

Tyke Tiler

✦ Answer these questions about Tyke Tiler.

✦ Name two good things Tyke did.

1 _____

2 _____

✦ Draw a picture of what you think Tyke might look like.

✦ Name two bad things Tyke did.

1 _____

2 _____

✦ Do you like Tyke? Write down your reasons why or why not, referring to the story.
_____
_____
_____

✦ Why do you think Tyke helps Danny all the time? Would you like Tyke for a friend?
_____
_____

✦ Why do you think Tyke wanted to ring the school bell?
_____
_____

Activity 3   **Name** _____

Tyke Tiler

◆ Answer the questions about Tyke Tiler in the boxes.

◆ What kind of person is Tyke Tiler? Describe Tyke's personality.	◆ Do you think Tyke is a good friend to Danny? Explain why, referring to the story.
◆ The Headmaster says Tyke is " . . . a disobedient, under-educated, under-disciplined, loud-mouthed ruffian . . . " but not a liar. Do you agree? Explain why or why not.	◆ Of Tyke and Danny, Mrs Somers said "That pair are troublemakers." Do you agree? Say why or why not.
◆ Tyke often considers the unfairness of life. Give one example from the story in which you think Tyke was treated unfairly and give your reasons why.	◆ Why do you think Tyke wanted to ring the school bell? 

Using Stories   Photocopiable
KS2: Y5–6/P6–7

Stories by the same author

Overall aims

+ To compare works by the same author.
+ To write a book 'blurb' for a back cover.

Featured books

Goggle Eyes and **Bill's New Frock**
by Anne Fine

Story synopses: Both stories have a school setting but are very different tales. *Bill's New Frock* is a lighthearted look at the differences in the ways boys and girls are treated. Bill wakes up one day to find he's a girl and the story tells of the problems he encounters. *Goggle Eyes* is a more serious look at the problems faced by children whose divorced parents meet another partner. It is a detailed account of a girl's reaction to a new adult family member.

LESSON ONE

Intended learning

+ To write a comparison between two books by the same author, supported by teacher modelling.

Starting point

+ Read the two stories to the class before this lesson so the children are familiar with them. They will also need to have selected two books of their own choice by their favourite author for the lesson. Explain that they are to compare the books they have chosen, using an activity sheet which asks them to consider differences and similarities. To help them, you are going to go through some of the same questions with them in relation to Anne Fine's books, *Goggle Eyes* and *Bill's New Frock*. Explain that this will give them practise in answering the questions and will provide them with an idea of the kinds of answers required. Discuss some of the questions from the activity sheets in detail. For example: Are the story settings similar in any way? Discuss the term 'setting' and what it means. In this case, both stories have a school setting. Do the children think the story is set in the past, present or future in the books? Ask them to support their answer by referring to the story. Are the settings realistic or imaginary. Ask them to explain their choices.

Using the differentiated activity sheets

Explain to the children that they are now to consider the two books they have selected in the same way.

Activity sheet 1

This is aimed at those children who have difficulty in making written responses. They may need help to read the questions and scribe some of the answers.

Activity sheet 2

This is aimed at more independent writers.

Activity sheet 3

This is aimed at more able children who can compare the author's approaches in more detail.

Plenary session

Bring the class together again. What difficulties did they have? Which questions did they find more challenging? Why? Go over these questions and provide suitable solutions to help them feel more confident about tackling similar work in the future. Finally, discuss the authors – why did the children select this particular author? What do they enjoy most about the author's style and subject matter?

Stories by the same author

◆ LESSON TWO ◆

◆ Intended learning

✦ To write a book 'blurb' to a pre-determined word limit
✦ To compare work with other pupil's and published versions.

◆ Starting point

✦ Ask the children to select four books, written by the same author, which they know really well. They should place these in front of them, face up. They are to pretend that they are the publicity agent for this author and that it is now their job to sell the books to as many people as they can!
✦ Working in pairs, they should select one of the books and in two minutes tell their partner all the good things about the story - tell them to imagine that their partner is a very wealthy client and if they can convince them that the book is brilliant, the client will buy lots of books.
✦ After each partner has had their turn, ask the children to return to their places to discuss the results. Who was convinced by their partner that the story was a good one? Why were they convinced? What made it sound so good?

Compare this with advertising and how adverts use flowery or exciting words to sell the product.

◆ Activity

✦ Ask the children to turn over three of the books on their desk so that the back covers are now showing and to read the book 'blurbs' telling them about the stories. Do they think one of them is particularly well written? Ask several children to read out examples. What do the others think? Would this make them want to read the book? Why or why not? Look how the blurbs are presented – some give a summary of the story, some provide an extract from the book, some mention the author's other books and/or awards, some give quotations from book reviewers. Which type of blurb do the children think works the best? Why? Ask them to read out an example of each type for others to compare. Are the blurbs for the same author similar or different? Why might this be?

✦ Now tell them that it is their task as agent to write the blurb for the fourth book on their desk. Tell them not to turn this one over to the back cover! It should make the book look really exciting to the reader and make them want to read the book. Tell them they are limited to 100 words. Encourage them to use a thesaurus to find appropriate words.

◆ Plenary session

When the children have completed the task, ask them to compare their blurb with the one actually written on the book's back cover. Which one do they prefer? Why? Ask some of them to read out their work to the class. Ask others to say constructive things about it. Discuss how difficult it was to keep to a word limit.

How important are book blurbs? How many children actually read them before selecting a book? What is the first thing they read when selecting a book? Why? Finally, ask them to change their blurb if necessary in the light of the discussions and produce a final copy to be displayed in the reading corner or library for others to read..

Stories by the same author

USING THE PHOTOCOPIABLE SHEETS AS A STIMULUS FOR FURTHER WORK

- Use the sheets as the backbone for writing a comparative essay comparing works by the same author.

- Use the information to write book reviews for a magazine.

- Use the information to prepare a talk to the rest of the class about the work of a particular author.

- Use the information to build up an author study.

- Write a letter from the main character in one story to the main character in another, commenting on how the author has treated them, what changes they would have made if they had written the story and so on.

OTHER IDEAS FOR USING STORIES BY THE SAME AUTHOR

- Make a poster of characters you meet in the books with a sentence describing each one. Display in reading corner to tempt others to read the books.

- Write letters from one character to another.

- Make a book about the author and the stories with background information on the author's life, a list of books written and a synopsis of the books. Use this as a reference guide in the school library.

- Compare the characters in the stories – do some reoccur? Are the characters by this author similar or very different?

- Make a television commercial which extols the virtues of the author and the books.

- Compare settings and plots. Is there a recurrent theme? Do the books end in similar ways? Is there always a problem to be solved?

- Study the language used by the author. Collect examples from texts which illustrate particular strengths of the author, such as use of metaphor, humour and suspense.

- Make up a play using characters from different books – make sure the dialogue is appropriate for each character.

- Write an ABC about this author – A is for *Angel of Nitshill Road*, B is for baffled, the way Bill felt, C is for the comfort Kitty gave to Helen (Anne Fine).

- Make mobiles to hang in the reading corner with the author's name at the top and separate cards for each book title, with a book review of each.

Activity 1   **Name** _____

◆ Stories by the same author ◆

Author _____
Book titles   1 _____
              2 _____

Setting

Are the story settings	similar ☐	different ☐
Is the setting in book 1	real ☐	imaginary ☐
Is the setting in book 2	real ☐	imaginary ☐
Is book 1 set in the	present ☐ past ☐	future ☐
Is book 2 set in the	present ☐ past ☐	future ☐

Story beginning

Which story beginning do you like best?   book 1 ☐   book 2 ☐

Why?   it is more exciting ☐

        it is easy to read ☐

        it makes me think something strange will happen ☐

Characters

Draw the two main characters. Tick boxes to describe each character.

[drawing box]	brave ☐ funny ☐ sad ☐ happy ☐ lonely ☐ frightened ☐ clever ☐
[drawing box]	brave ☐ funny ☐ sad ☐ happy ☐ lonely ☐ frightened ☐ clever ☐

Plot

Write yes or no

Could the story be true?   book 1 ☐   book 2 ☐

Did you enjoy the ending?   book 1 ☐   book 2 ☐

Does the story have a message?   book 1 ☐   book 2 ☐

Using Stories   Photocopiable

Activity 2 Name _____

✦ Stories by the same author ✦

Author _____

Book titles   1 _____

    2 _____

Setting   Are the story settings similar in any ways? In what ways?
_____
_____

   Are the settings realistic or imaginary? Explain your choices.
_____
_____

Story beginning   Compare how the stories begin. Which beginning do you prefer?
       Give your reasons.
_____
_____
_____

Characters   Write down one word which best describes the main character in each story.
       Beside the word explain why you have chosen it for that character.
_____

   Are the main characters in these stories similar in any way?
   Explain why or why not.
_____
_____

Plot   How true to life are the events that happen? Why do you think the
       author wrote these stories?
_____
_____
_____

✦ Use the back of this page to write down which book you enjoyed the most.
 Explain your opinion as fully as you can, referring to the story.

Activity 3   **Name** _____

◆ Stories by the same author ◆

Author _____

Book titles   1 _____
              2 _____

Setting   Compare the settings in the two books. Comment on how realistic you think they are.

_____
_____
_____
_____
_____

Story beginning   Compare the story beginnings. Use extracts from the books to support
                   your comments.

_____
_____
_____
_____
_____

Characters   Explain how the author's choice of words and phrases helps to create
              a vivid impression of what the main characters are like.
              Compare the approach used in each book.

_____
_____
_____
_____
_____

Plot   Which story do you prefer? How does the author make you sympathise
        with this story? Explain your opinion, using extracts from the story.

_____
_____
_____
_____
_____

Using Stories   Photocopiable
KS2: Y5–6/P6–7

Acknowledgements

The following is a list of all the children's storybooks that have been referred to in this book as the basis for literacy work.

- ◆ *Witches* by Roald Dahl (Puffin, 1983)

- ◆ *The Eighteenth Emergency* by Betsy Byars (Puffin 1973)

- ◆ *The Lion, the Witch and the Wardrobe* by C S Lewis (Collins, 1980)

- ◆ *Roald Dahl's James and the Giant Peach: A Play* adapted by Richard R George (Puffin, 1982)

- ◆ *The Orchard Book of Fairy Tales* retold by Rose Impey (Orchard Books, 1994)

- ◆ *Grimm's Fairy Tales* translated by Peter Carter (Oxford University Press, 1997)

- ◆ *Snow White and the Seven Dwarfs* retold by Jenny Koralek (Macdonald Young Books, 1997)

- ◆ *Snow White in New York* by Fiona French (Oxford University Press, 1991) Used by permission of Oxford University Press

- ◆ *Aesop's Fables* retold by Jacqueline Morley (Macdonald Young Books, 1995)

- ◆ *A Thief in the Village and Other Stories* by James Berry (Puffin, 1989)

- ◆ *Smith* by Leon Garfield (Puffin, 1981)

- ◆ *Goosebumps: The Curse of the Mummy's Tomb* by R L Stine (Scholastic Inc, 1993)

- ◆ *Elephants Don't Sit on Cars* by David Henry Wilson (Macmillan Children's Books, 1996)

- ◆ *Esio Trot* by Roald Dahl (Puffin 1991)

- ◆ *The Bully* by Jan Needle (Puffin 1995)

- ◆ *The Angel of Nitshill Road* by Anne Fine (Mammoth 1993)

- ◆ *The Turbulent Term of Tyke Tiler* by Gene Kemp (Puffin 1979)

- ◆ *Goggle Eyes* by Anne Fine (Puffin 1990)

- ◆ *Bill's New Frock* by Anne Fine (Mammoth Books 1990)